The Gold Necklace

by
Willadine Bain

The author has tried to recreate events, locales and conversations from her memories of them. In some instances she may have changed some identifying characteristics and details such as physical properties, occupations and places of residence.

Cover design by Jennifer Deslaurier, Notus Publishing
Photos are from the private collections of Willadine Bain and Coralie Barksdale unless otherwise noted

Printed in the United States of America
First Printing, 2019

ISBN 9781692849160

Notus Publishing
www.NotusBooks.com

In this book, you will read about the phenomenal rise of Willadine Bain's family from slavery to include one of the country's first black millionaires, and how she became the first African American teacher to write, produce and appear in Philadelphia's new educational TV market.

Along the way, you will see pictures of how the family interacted with luminaries such as United States Senator Edward Brooke, Guion Bluford, the first African American astronaut to step on the moon, former US Ambassador to France Pamela Harriman and renowned African American architect Phil Freelon. Freelon designed the most recent Smithsonian Museum of African American History and Culture in Washington, DC.

These stories remind us of the hundreds of thousands of former slaves who developed skills and qualities of leadership to help our country in the past, present and future. You will also hear the story of the purchase of a beaded gold necklace that has been worn by four generations of educators in the family. We hope that you enjoy "The Gold Necklace."

This book is dedicated to:
Philip Freelon, Architect
My beloved husband, Norbert
My children, Norbert and Coralie
My grandchildren, Greg and Rachel
My grandfather, Franklin Jones

My humble thanks to the skillful and dedicated editing and contribution of ideas and outlooks from my daughter, Coralie Barksdale, and personal historian Barbara Sherf.

Table of Contents

Chapter One
Grandmother Adele – Born to Slavery

I believe that my earliest ancestor was a young African woman who, torn from her home, arrived in bondage on American shores in the early 1800s. I think of her as beautiful, strong, resourceful and full of hope. Purchased by a plantation owner, she was put to work in the hot fields of Georgia. Her story and those of her children stretches onward through the hundreds of years of our nation's history – until the third and fourth generation.

Adela, her daughter, was born a slave in the state of Georgia in the year 1825. She did not plant cotton in the wide fields of the plantation. She lived in a little log cabin near the Big House where she sewed for the other slaves and their children, and sometimes for the Master and his family. It was in this way that she came in contact with the Master's son, and he became the father of her two daughters, Adele and Letitia. The small family continued to live in their own little cabin even though there was no insulation and the dirt floor was often cold.

On one sunny day, when little Adele and her sister were playing with friends outside of the cabin, they suddenly heard a great booming, pounding noise! They took off running to the edge of the field where they lived, climbed a tall fence at the end of the property, and looked far off into the distance across the water to see the high buildings of a city far away. Atlanta was engulfed in flames! The girls heard guns crackling and cannons thundering! Smoke was shooting up, streaking the sky!

When their mother came to find them she cried, "See the smoke way out there? That's the city of Atlanta! It is burning, and when General Sherman and his men come and take Atlanta, we will all be free, and we will never be slaves again!"

On New Year's Day 1863, as the nation approached its third year of the bloody Civil War between the North and South, President Abraham Lincoln issued the Emancipation Proclamation. The proclamation declared, "All persons held as slaves within the rebellious states are and henceforth shall be free!"

After years of bitter conflict, the Civil War was finally over! Adele and her sister Letitia, their mother, Adela, and the slaves of the American South raised their voices in one great cry, "We are free at last!"

Their former Master bought Adela and her family a small house near the city of Savannah, Georgia, where free people of color were beginning to live.

Adela continued to work as a seamstress for wealthy customers and other people in the city --both black and white.

Adele and Letitia attended Beach Institute, the first public school in America built to educate newly freed African American children. Quaker women from the North were their teachers. The school was newly built, although the books were few. Adele and Letitia studied hard and graduated from Beach Institute in 1876 with the equivalent of a high school diploma.

Adele earned a scholarship to attend a new college for African Americans called Atlanta University. It sat high on a hill above the growing city of Atlanta, Georgia. She graduated in 1880 and became one of first black public school teachers in America!

Adele applied to become a teacher in one of the newly opened schools for colored children in her hometown of Savannah, Georgia. Her school was not far from her home, and she enjoyed dressing up and meeting the children every day.

Adele made a pretty new dress to wear in her classroom and bought a silver comb to hold up her heavy black hair. She also bought a bright, pink umbrella to shield her fair skin from the sun as she walked from the family home across the railroad tracks to the school every day.

One day, as she walked across the railroad tracks on her way to school, a smartly dressed young white gentleman with twinkling blue eyes and curly brown hair stopped Adele on her way to school. He asked to carry her umbrella. She was startled! She knew of the attacks of white boys against Negro girls in the South. But the young man was cordial and chatted with enthusiasm. Adele realized that he did not know she was a Negro. She continued to rebuff his advances. The young man was crestfallen when she turned and walked away at the next street.

On another day, the dark-haired boy appeared, waiting at the street corner as Adele went by. The boy begged to walk with her on her way home from school. This pattern continued for some time. He was smitten! And so was Adele!

They confided in each other as they continued to meet. The young man invited her to his plush home to meet his parents. And so they were married.

It was a happy time at first. The young gentleman's parents were glad to see him settle down with a lovely and talented girl. But soon the restless young man began to drift. He traveled on sailing ships with shady gamblers. At times he won, but when he did not, his temper flared. One night, a shot rang out from his ship as it was anchored in the port! The lights on the deck blinked three times – meaning a crime had been committed at sea! Apparently there had been a dispute over the winnings on the boat. Adele's husband and another man participated in a duel over the disputed money. Adele's husband did not win the match. He died of a gunshot wound!

Panicked and alone, Adele fled the plush household and returned to her mother's home. No more was said. She returned to her classroom with a broken heart. Using some of the money she had earned while teaching, Adele bought a beautiful, solid gold beaded necklace so that she would always remember this time in her life.

Chapter Two
Grandfather Franklin Jones – A Slave with a Future

I was six years old when I first met my maternal grandfather, Franklin Jones. He was 83 years old and had come to Philadelphia from his home in Savannah, Georgia, to visit his daughter, my mother, Mildred Grinnage, and my father, Dr. Willard Grinnage, at our house on 2324 Christian Street.

When grandfather first came to our house, I had to look way up at him. He must have been over 6-feet tall. I remember he wore a gray suit and a wide, flat gray hat. His skin was smooth and brown and when he looked at me and smiled, his eyes twinkled. From the start, I knew we were going to be great friends!

Every day after dinner, Grandfather Jones would say, "Okay, Scout, let's take a walk and see what's going on in the world." He would put on his hat, take an apple from the kitchen table, and out the door we would go. We'd walk down the block and sit on the marble steps that were in front of every home. He would take out his penknife and cut juicy pieces of apple for both of us.

I would tell him stories about my cats and he would tell me about some of the things that had happened to him when he was my age.

Grandfather told me that he was born in a very Big House on a plantation where cotton and corn grew. He and his little brother were born on the same day. The only difference was that his brother's skin was white and grandfather's skin was dark brown. Their father was the Master of the large plantation. Grandfather said that he and his brother slept, ate and played together every day. They were loved by all of the family in the Big House and especially by their white grandmother who often took them riding in her gold-trimmed carriage.

However, when the boys were 7 years old, grandfather's white brother was sent to school in a town far away and Franklin was left at home alone. His heart was broken! He cried! He had lost his best friend! The housekeepers on the plantation gave him little jobs, but he ran away and hid in the barn. The cook tied a brown apron around Franklin's neck and gave him work to do in the kitchen. But it was noisy and full of big people, and Franklin ran away again and again. His grandmother drove her carriage all over the farm to find him. When he was finally discovered and returned, he was whipped, dressed in a brown potato sack like other Negro boys on the farm and sent to the fields to pick cotton.

Franklin was always running away, being punished, and brought back--until he was a boy of 14. Then, one night he hid in a loaded wagon, waited until dark, jumped off and ran into the deep forest. He kept running, day and night, eating berries and stealing bird's eggs for food. For many weeks he traveled on with a heavy heart.

One day he came to a clearing in the forest where he saw a group of Negro men all dressed in blue uniforms sitting around a fire. He asked them for food and water.

They told him they were soldiers in the Black Unit of the Union Army under the President of the United States, whose name was Abraham Lincoln. They had joined the Union Army to fight the Confederate soldiers and put an end to slavery.

"Were you a slave?" they asked. "You were brave to run away!"

The soldiers invited Franklin to join them. Even though he was only 14 years old, he was tall and strong. He joined his fellow black soldiers of the Union Army, and traveled miles across the South, fighting many battles under their great General whose name was Sherman.

By the time the "Great War to End Slavery" was over in 1865, about 200,000 black men had served in the United States Army. Ninety thousand of them had been former slaves like my grandfather.

After the Civil War, Grandfather said that it was a great day when he arrived at the old marketplace near his former home on the plantation, and jumped off the truck, wearing his Union Army blue uniform with flashy brass buttons! Although he was not really a Captain, the people cheered and called him, "Captain Jones." They wanted to hear about the big battles and how the cannons rolled and the horses leaped forward with flags flying!

Just then, as if by a miracle, Franklin's beloved white grandmother came riding in her carriage into the marketplace to meet him. She hugged him and a great celebration began! His grandmother found a free Negro man who owned a meat store where she had often shopped. She asked the storeowner to take Franklin into his store and teach him the business. And he did!

Franklin worked long hours in the store and grew to admire the owner. They expanded the business by selling food to black and white families – rich and poor. When the owner died, he left the meat market to Franklin.

The market flourished as the city grew! After many years, Franklin opened a large meat and produce market in a place called the "Cotton Exchange," in the center of the flourishing city of Savannah. This market distributed foreign and local products all over the South. It flourished for the next 30 years, and grandfather became one of Savannah's first African American millionaires! The year was 1870.

The thriving Frank Jones market became a familiar meeting place for affluent businessmen, black and white. Grandfather married, settled down and bought a new house for his growing family in a modest black neighborhood.

(He and his first wife had three daughters. One of them married Stanley Neal, and their daughter, Elizabeth, married Allan Freelon, Jr. Their children were Randi, Gregory, Philip, and Douglas.)

Successful African American businessmen, with whom grandfather fraternized in the Cotton Exchange, began to invite him to join them in social and business affairs. Once they invited him to St. Luke's Episcopal Church, which was frequented by newly prosperous African American families.

Grandfather told me that one Sunday, dressed in his best linen suit and flat, black hat, he presented his six-foot, four-inch frame at the great red door of St. Luke's Church. He said he got a good "looking over" by the ushers at the door, but was allowed to enter. He found a seat in the middle of the enormous, high-ceilinged church. The flying flags, the tall golden cross, and thundering organ astounded him!

A lace-robed African American boy escorted a golden cross down the aisle. Grandfather was amazed by the scent of the swinging pot of incense held by a beautiful black lady in a sweeping dress. But the incense made him sneeze. Franklin took out a large cloth from his pocket and proceeded to blow his nose loudly. He noticed that the girls sitting near him in the pew were giggling, and realized that instead of a white handkerchief, he had taken out a red table napkin from home. Hastily, he stuffed the napkin in his pocket and lowered his eyes in discomfort.

Despite this amazing breach of protocol, the twittering young church ladies who sat near him invited Mr. Jones, who it was rumored had made a large fortune in the food market business, to tea and cakes after church. Franklin was especially impressed with a fair-skinned, blue-eyed young lady in a pink hat who was a member of the church. A courtship ensued and Franklin turned over his business empire to his sons, divorced his current wife, and married Adele Kendall in the year 1890. He bought her a grand house on Peach Tree Street in Savannah -- two stories high, surrounded by double porches. He also bought her a great carriage driven by a man named Joe.

Over the years one of the visitors to her home was W.E.B. Du Bois, co-founder of the NAACP. He and Adele would debate the value of a college education versus the value of going to trade school; a debate Du Bois often had with Booker T. Washington.

In 1893, their daughter, my Aunt Eleanor was born, and in 1895, my mother Mildred. Franklin took the family on many trips to Canada, New York, and the Jersey shore. The girls grew up and attended college. Eleanor went to Atlanta University, where she received a degree in home economics. My mother, Mildred Jones, went to Howard University in Washington, DC, and received a Bachelor's Degree in Education. She happily married the love of her life-- Willard Grinnage, a Howard dental student.

I learned so much from Grandfather Jones! Despite the actions of his own white father who stripped him of his fine clothes, his toys, and his playmate brother, Grandfather made a great success of his life. He knew that his father had followed the Southern tradition that ensured that a family fortune could not fall to a black descendant. His brother had been sent away to school to prepare him to inherit the family fortune. Grandfather never regretted that he ran away from home, but he never forgot his grandmother who inspired him to recover his life.

Born in 1845, maternal Grandfather "Captain" Frank Jones, went from a slave to fighting in the Union Army to becoming a successful businessman in in Savannah, Georgia.

Maternal Grandmother Adele Jones was born in Savannah in 1855. She attended Beach Institute, a school for the children of freed slaves, and was in the first graduating class at Atlanta University. She became an elementary school teacher and married Frank Jones in 1875.

A photo of Dr. Willard Grinnage's first dental office at 20th and Dickinson Streets in Philadelphia in 1924.

The longtime family home and dental offices at 2324 Christian Street in South Philadelphia.

On the boardwalk with Mom, a family friend, and Dad during one of the many family trips.

Willadine, 11, with her father, Dr. Willard Grinnage, posing in front of his new car!

In the center is Willadine, 14, surrounded by Girls' High School friends Bettina Amonetti (left) and Gloria Bullock.

Founders' Library at Howard University

Willadine is all smiles at Howard University's Graduation Day in 1947!

On a date at the beach with Howard University Dental School student Norbert Bain.

20

Willadine, 26, marries Howard University Dental School graduate ('34) Norbert Bain on December 27, 1950 at St. Simon's Church. The reception was held at The Pyramid Club. The photograph was taken by renowned photographer John W. Mosely. Another photo by Moseley, of Willadine in her wedding gown, was displayed at an exhibit of his work at the Woodmere Art Museum in Chestnut Hill.

Norbert Bain II was born December 21, 1953, and daughter Coralie (Corie) is born February 13, 1955. This is a photo of their father reading stories to them.

Corie receives a nice kiss from brother "Nubs" outside of grandparents' home and dental offices on Christening Day.

The family moved to their home at 335 W. Sedgwick Street in 1957.

Family Christmas photo with matching sleepwear!

Confirmation Day for the boys (from left) Wayne Reid, Phil Freelon, Norbert "Nubs" Bain, who are celebrating with Penny Norris, Pam Norris, Melissa Reid and Randi (Freelon) Vega.

Coralie's Confirmation Celebration with friends (from left) Carl (Reggie) Johnson, Coralie, Donita White, and Byron Brooks.

24

Willadine starts as an English teacher and winds up under the bright lights at WHYY and Channel 3 in Philadelphia, producing and appearing in three educational programs for children.

Norbert's Wedding Day! Norbert is seen here with (from left) Allan Freelon, Cel Bernardino, Phil Freelon, his lovely bride, Natalie Bain, Dr. Norbert Bain, Willadine Bain, Dr. Gregory Barksdale, Coralie Barksdale and Val Hawkins. A good time was had by all!

Coralie marries Dr. Gregory Barksdale on February 16, 1974. Seen here with the bride and groom, from left to right are Deborah Mike, Cynthiana (Cindy) Lightfoot, Dr. Norbert Bain, Willadine, Bette Barksdale, Kedric Barksdale, Barry Lenoir, Esq., and Norbert Bain.

26

Known as the "Four Sisters" because of their lifelong friendship that began at Camp Atwater are (from left to right) Wallette Lynch, Penny Norris, Willadine Bain and Emily Robertson at one of many celebrations!

The late US Senator Edward Brooke was photographed with Wallette Lynch and Willadine Bain at the wedding of Amy and Al Goldson in Martha's Vineyard.

Social clubs and organizations are very important in the African American community in Philadelphia. This picture was taken at the Commissioner's Dance where Dr. Bain was a longtime member. Dr. Willard Grinnage was one of the founders of this club of prominent, professional African American men. Seen here are Dr. and Mrs. Norbert Bain, and Dr. Gregory and Coralie Barksdale.

Astronaut Guion Bluford, the first African American astronaut to travel into space, explained his work to Greg Barksdale and other young people. Dr. and Mrs. Norbert Bain had the opportunity to celebrate his success at a party that was given by Coralie Barksdale's Godmother and Bluford's aunt, Jean Bluford.

28

Willadine (center) is the only surviving charter member of the the Circle-Lets Philadelphia Chapter, a social club of women. She and her daughter, Coralie (far right) are current members of the club whose members are pictured here. Willadine also enjoys membership in the Links, the Karma Club, several bridge clubs and the Birthday Girls Club!

Friends Bill and Cindy Lightfoot spending time with us at the Greenbrier Resort at a Circle-Let's Conclave in Roanoke. The couple introduced Coralie and Gregory.

Wesley Brown (second from right) was the first African American to graduate from the US Naval Academy. Others tried before him, but were drummed out due to racism and segregation. In four years, the only person who spoke to Wes Brown while he was in the Naval Academy was Jimmy Carter, future President of the United States. The Navy built the Wesley Brown Fieldhouse at the Naval Academy in Annapolis, Maryland to honor his accomplishments. Willadine is a very good friend of his widow, Crystal Brown. As a young girl, Willadine resided with Aunt Crystal's mother, Mrs. Malone, during most of her time at Howard University. Crystal Brown is on the left, and friend Betty Dixon is center.

The Ambassador's Ball in Paris, France with (from left) Willadine Bain, Pamela Harriman, two Washington D.C. friends and Bettina (Amonetti) Nicholas. They attended a soiree hosted by Ambassador Harriman. Other guests included Dr. Norbert Bain, Dr. and Mrs. Tanner McMahon, Wes and Crystal Brown and Dr. Nina Nicholas.

30

The Philmont Country Club was the venue to honor Central High School graduates who have done exceptional work in their fields. Pictured here are (bottom row) Willadine Bain, the late Phil Freelon, a renowned architect, and Coralie Barksdale. Top row (from left to right) are Dr. Greg Barksdale, Harry Drummond, and Greg Barksdale, Jr. Phil, who passed in July 2019, was honored for his stellar career in architecture that includes his most recent accomplishment as the lead architect whose firm designed the National Smithsonian Museum of African American History and Culture.

Willadine and her "Story Corner" colleagues get together for a fun reunion!

The next generation carries on with Rachael Bain and Greg Barksdale who are seen here relaxing at a family celebration!

Chapter Three
Willard Grinnage - Let Me Tell You About My Father

My father's father, Willard Grinnage, was a member of the Great Blackhawk Indian Nation that dominated the rich agricultural fields of central Georgia, before they were destroyed and driven away by white settlers in the late 1800s. Like many of his tribe, Willard Grinnage followed the long road north, and finally settled in the quiet farmlands of Delaware. There he struggled to plant and cultivate a small plot of land rented from a white farm owner, built a little house and tried to begin again. He married Reba, a pretty, mixed-race Indian and Negro woman.

Side by side the couple tilled the fields on their tiny farm. Reba went each week to sew for ladies in the nearby town of Wilmington in order to help the family to survive.

My father, Willard Grinnage, Jr., was born in 1884. He grew up on the farm working and playing. At the age of 12, he was almost as tall as his father. A snapshot shows a sturdy fellow, with red brown skin, black curly hair and a bright, direct smile. He is wearing old work pants, a plaid shirt, a floppy brimmed hat, and is carrying a long gun over his shoulder.

When Willard was not helping his father plow and cultivate their small plot of land, he spent occasional days at a school for colored children not far from his home in the Wilmington area. Young Willard became friendly with the many Negro boys who combined school and work in the way that he did. Many were poor. Some had parents who were shopkeepers and businesspeople. One such fortunate student was named Roland Milburne. He was the nephew of a black pharmacist, who owned a drugstore in town. The boys became fast friends. As Willard grew, he found his school time more and more exhilarating. He met boys from many places he had never heard of – East Orange, Atlantic City, and even Philadelphia! He loved being a part of his new school family and stayed on the farm less and less. Studying arithmetic, reading, agriculture and American History, he read books about people in countries far away. And he learned to play football! With rules!

When the boys were about 16 and had completed the first years of schooling, Willard's best friend, Roland Milburne announced that he was going away to another school. He was going to college!

"College," he said, "was a very big school with many, many buildings and students from towns and cities far away." The name of this big school was Howard University, which was founded in 1867 as a federally chartered, private, coeducational, historically black university in Washington, DC.

Students could stay in the dormitory, eat their food there, and even sleep there every night. If they passed a certain test they could start in what was called the Howard Undergraduate Class. Willard was amazed! He told his parents and begged to go to the big new school to continue his education. His mother explained that they had no money and his father needed him on the farm. Young Willard was broken-hearted.

That autumn, when crops were low, Willard set off for Atlantic City, New Jersey. He had heard that men and boys could earn money there pushing rolling chairs on a long boardwalk beside the Atlantic Ocean. In this way Willard hoped to save enough money to go to Howard University and start his college education. But after a month of work, the quarters he had earned pushing chairs never seemed to be enough.

One day when he was puffing and pushing a rolling chair past the painted stores on the boardwalk, who should rush up and throw his arms around him but his friend Milburne! He and his uncle were taking a vacation at the shore before college started.

Milburne had a bright idea!

"Why don't you come with me to Washington?" he asked. "You could buy a train ticket with the money you've saved. And when you get there you could stay with me in the house for boys called the dormitory, and no one will know that you aren't a real student."

"But where will I sleep?" Willard asked.

"You can sleep under my bed and no one will know you're there," Milburne responded.

And he did!

The dormitory at Howard was full of young men, some much older than Willard, who like him had left school and jobs and entered Howard in the hope of earning a college education. They were from places with strange names like Rhode Island, Massachusetts, and even Trinidad, West Indies. Wrapped in a blanket, Willard slept under Milburne's bed and attended classes where African American and white professors told exciting stories about a world he never knew. He listened and studied and began to grasp the information that the professors gave. But one night, the dormitory matron came to Milburne's room. She told Willard that he had not paid his tuition and that he had to pack up and go home.

With tears in his eyes, Willard told the matron about the hopes and dreams of his family. The matron asked what Willard could do to earn money for the tuition that Howard required? Willard could think of only one thing he could do really well and that was play football. He had heard that Howard University needed some strong boys for the growing undergraduate football program. He applied to become a member and was given a temporary football scholarship and permission to join the freshman undergraduate class, provided he maintained satisfactory grades. The year was 1913.

Willard eagerly began the Howard freshman year, studying algebra, physical science, world history and English grammar. He attended lectures and joined discussion groups. He played football and became captain of the team. He also waited tables in the cafeteria. Later he would be part of the wait staff at fancy restaurants and would bring home leftovers for his hungry fraternity brothers.

In his senior year at Howard, Willard met and fell in love with a beautiful African American Southern belle with fair-skin, gray eyes, and coal black hair. Her name was Mildred Jones. She and her smiling, fluttering girlfriends had entered the freshman class.

In June 1915, Willard completed his undergraduate studies at the age of 21. His incredulous parents came to see him graduate from the Howard University Undergraduate School with degrees in Physical Science and Physical Education.

Now came the time for joyous conversation among Willard and his four classmates concerning possible enrollment in the Howard Professional Schools the next year. Milburne wanted to study pharmacy, and Walter Garvin wanted to be a dentist. Merrill Curtis was going to study medicine, as his father was a physician. All of the families would somehow find ways to pay for this wonderful opportunity to step into a new world of highly lucrative, individual entrepreneurship and science.

Willard's family had no money to support him in continuing his education. He decided to make an impassioned plea to the Dean of Howard's Dental School. In exchange for a four-year scholarship, he would play full-time on the Howard University Varsity Football team and would secure a job to pay for incidentals and supplies.

The Dean met with the Advisory Board. They considered Willard's excellent scholastic average and his past admirable performance as Captain of the football team.

(Perhaps they knew that the Howard team would soon play the highly rated Carlisle Indians, the Champions of the

West Coast Black Football League, whose hero was Jim Thorpe!)

The Board finally voted to grant Mr. Grinnage a four-year scholarship to the Howard University School of Dental Medicine, provided that he maintained an acceptable grade point average. He was authorized to play full-time on Howard's Varsity football team for the duration of his time in school.

Willard now began the long, grinding years of professional study, but his spirit soared when he crashed through the lines and heard the crowds roar!

It was said that sometimes, when Willard was injured and brought from the field on a stretcher, he would lift up his blanket and wink at the screaming co-eds who followed him as he was carried from the field!

After four years of work and study and friendship, Willard graduated from the Howard University School of Dentistry in 1918 with a degree in Dental Surgery, scoring an A in Organic Chemistry. He was the first in his family to receive an education.

Soon after graduation, Willard was drafted into the segregated United States Army. He served until the end of WW I.

Upon his return home in 1923, Willard married his Howard University sweetheart, Mildred Jones from Savannah, Georgia. The couple moved to Philadelphia, and with the help of his affluent Father-in-Law, Frank Jones, Willard opened his first dental office at 20th and Catherine Streets in South Philadelphia. Willard Grinnage was one of the first three African American dentists to practice in Philadelphia and his practice was an immediate success.

In 1925, Dr. Grinnage and his wife Mildred, now a school teacher, bought a three-story home with white marble steps, a big bay window, an office on the second floor, and an apartment on the third floor, in what was then a fashionable area of Philadelphia, at 23rd and Christian Streets.

In the 1930s, the Great Depression caused restrictions to the practice of dentistry. My father continued his practice but was also employed by the Roosevelt Administration as Director of The Fair Employment Practices Commission. The Commission secured jobs for many talented young black citizens in the region. In the 1940s, he decided to run for public office.

According to a Howard University alumni newsletter the following excerpt was included:

"Reliable information has reached us that Dr. Grinnage has tossed his hat squarely in the middle of the ring with a definite likelihood of going to the Pennsylvania State Senate this spring. All old How-ardites will remember Grinnage from his line-smashing feats in football back in the "good old days." May we say in football parlance then, "hit 'em hard," Grinnage! Aside from being an active practitioner, Dr. Grinnage has shared an important role in developments in dentistry and social welfare. He is Past President of the Odonto Chirurgical Society, of Philadelphia, a dental organization, a member of the Executive Committee of the National Dental Association and an intense supporter of all projects for civic and community improvement."

However, Dr. Willard Grinnage did not win that election. He continued in his successful dental practice and was very socially involved in the community. He was one of the founders of the Philadelphia Commissioners, a social club and men's organization, which continues to thrive today. He was also a longtime member of the Pyramid Club.

Grandmother Reba Grinnage bought a small house around the corner from 2324 Christian Street, on a street called St. Alban's Place. She enjoyed being near her family. And she is the one who told me this story.

Chapter Four
Willadine Bain - My Story

I was born on May 22, 1926. As an only child, I had many happy memories filled with a diverse group of neighborhood friends on our block. My parents and I lived at 2324 Christian Street in South Philadelphia, which was then considered one of the most elite and diverse sections of the city. A large community of businessmen, architects, doctors, dentists, teachers and undertakers made their homes there. The many streets were wide and lined with a variety of red brick buildings, all with glistening white marble front steps.

Our home was in the middle of the block on a street that was filled with the laughter of children. It was three stories high and had a large, three-sided bay window on the second floor. It was the only house with a bay window.

On the ground in front of our house was a three-foot square sandstone step. Our front door was made of dark, shiny wood with a large glass window stating "Dentist" in bright gold letters. This door opened into a marble vestibule with steps leading into the house. My father's dental office, waiting room and family bedrooms were up the stairs on the second floor. Downstairs contained our living room, dining room, and kitchen. A third-floor apartment was for guests.

Our house was always full of children playing, laughing and calling to each other. On sunny days we played jacks, hopscotch, jump rope, hide-and-seek and tag on the pavement and on the neighbor's white marble steps. Sometimes we ran "down the corner" to Montrose Street. But we always ran right back screaming because, "Who knew what kind of kids lived around there?"

We played long games of Monopoly on the brown sandstone step in front of our front door. When the weather turned rainy, we picked up the game and played in our marble vestibule, or on the rug at the foot of the stairs until incoming patients made us move.

If the weather was bad, we asked Muriel, our helper, if we children could be allowed to go up the stairs to the front bedroom and enjoy looking out our big bay window to see the exciting traffic and people passing by.

Early in the morning, we might hear the clip-clop of hooves and see horses pulling a red wagon around the corner. The milkman would be ringing his bell and calling out, "Hey, Milk-a-Man! Come and get your fresh milk today!"

We might then see the Fishman rolling a big flat wagon of silvery fish down the street. He would walk along calling "Hey Fish-a-man here!" Then we would see women with kerchiefs tied around their heads coming out of the houses to look at the glistening, wriggly fish. They would ask the Fishman to scrape the scales off, weigh the fish, and wrap the purchase in newspaper to be taken home.

The Iceman could be seen getting off his truck with huge blocks of ice wrapped in burlap cloth, held tight on his shoulder. We watched, as he might be coming to our house with his ice pick to chop off a small block of ice for our icebox. Muriel might ask him to come into our kitchen so she could shave flakes of ice into folded cups for us and pour syrup over the ice chips as a treat before the block was returned to the icebox. We children would come tumbling down from the bedroom to sit around the kitchen table and enjoy our homemade sweet frozen treats!

Later we would run back upstairs to the bedroom and play "hide and seek" until Muriel chased the children home.

On our block, there were all kinds of children – black, white, Jewish, Christian and Muslim. My best friend was Shangle Goldberg, a 7-year-old Jewish girl who lived two doors down from me. She had wavy, red-brown hair that curled on your finger when you picked it up. Shangle usually brought her 4-year-old sister, Betty, when she came over to my house to play.

There was Temple Peacock, a chubby, pouty colored boy with wide eyes, who lived near us. He couldn't run fast, but he could shoot marbles – straight!

Lynne was the oldest. She had come all the way over the ocean in a boat from a place called Trinidad. Lynne always helped with the little kids, and she would make dolls out of cloth! She had a handsome older brother who always wanted to kiss me. But I wouldn't let him!

Elsie had long blonde hair and blue eyes. Sometimes she worked in her father's bakery at our corner.

Bobby Larken had just come from Ireland with his father, who wanted to find a job in America. Many people were poor in those days.

And there was a boy named Bennie who lived at the end of our street. We played with him sometimes, when we ran down there. He had a bad leg and pushed himself along on a wagon with his other leg. But he could throw a ball and catch too! We had fun playing with him, although he couldn't come up our way because of his leg. Bennie always smiled when he saw us coming.

We called ourselves "Our Gang" like the kids in the Little Rascals movies.

In the winter, when there was snow piled high on Christian Street, we climbed the three-foot piles of collected snow by the curb, and slid down the mounds screaming!

On bright days we would go down the block for a walk. Muriel, our helper, would tell us to be careful and Lynne would lead the way. We walked to all of the corner stores on Christian Street.

There was a candy store run by a plump Italian lady who would always smile when we came in. She might give us a licorice stick from a big glass jar by the front window. She had everything in that store! Chocolate pretzels, bubblegum, balloons, dolls, trains, comic books, jump ropes, school supplies and toys that jumped when you pulled the string. We looked at everything, but we only had a few cents to buy something.

At the pharmacy, we were sometimes given mints when we went to deliver our mother's prescriptions.
Across the street was Callahan's Irish Bar and Grille. It had smells of beer, sounds of loud music, and men going in and out.

Further on, was Elsie's father's German bakery. It always smelled of doughnuts and pies baking in the ovens. Elsie's mother might give us broken pieces of crullers and cookies wrapped in paper napkins to eat as we walked home.

After our walk, my mother might invite the gang down to the playroom in the basement of my house. She would give us lemonade, fruit and pretzels! We would dance, and sing songs like, "A tisket, a tasket, I lost my yellow basket!" And we'd dance until it was time for everyone to go home!

Sometimes when it was "Kid's Day" at the movies we would ask Muriel to take us all to the segregated Avon Theater on South Street to see a "Flash Gordon" movie. We had fun walking down the street holding hands. When we got to the movies, the ushers always told the white kids to sit on one side of the theater, and the colored kids to sit on the other side. When the lights went out, we would all jump into the middle seats and have a great time watching the movie together!

When I was 8 years old, my parents decided to send me to Stevens Practice School at 13th and Spring Garden Streets. It was a special school taught by master teachers. Their lessons served as demonstrations for student teachers who worked under them.

My friends, most of whose parents were professionals and businesspeople, all went to Stevens School together each morning in a big limousine owned by the Chew Funeral Director! All of my other classmates were white. I remember that my fourth-grade teacher, Mrs. Jones, always refused to shake my hand in line as we said goodbye at the end of the day. I was sad and told my mother. She went to the school and made a complaint to the teacher who was white. After that Mrs. Jones just stopped having any goodbye handshakes after class.

My best friend, Margaret, who was white, lived in a large house in Center City. Her mother's next-door neighbor was the famous writer, Pearl Buck. Margaret and I often went to the writer's house to play and see her wonderful things from China. I frequently went to Margaret's house to play, but her mother would not allow her to come to mine.

As a young teen, I went to Camp Atwater in beautiful East Brookfield, Massachusetts. The camp had a beautiful blue lake with a diving board and all kinds of activities including swimming, diving, rifle practice, baseball, theater and arts and crafts.

Many of the children of my parents' professional friends from all over the country went to Atwater Camp. The counselors were medical and dental students who came from African American universities across the country. I met campers Wallette Bolden from New York, Penny Norris from New Jersey, Emily Robertson from Boston, Eloise Allen and girls from states all across the country. It was wonderful. These friendships have lasted throughout my adult life.

The Great Depression

At this time, newspapers began printing gloomy reports about the national economy. There were shortages of food in the markets. Coal was becoming scarce. Some of my father's patients began to have trouble paying their bills. They brought him sacks of potatoes and bags of coal that they had picked up along the railroad tracks on Point Breeze Avenue to use as payment for their dental work.

The year was 1929 and radio announcers proclaimed that President Herbert Hoover had declared a National Emergency!

My father and his friend and neighbor Thomas Goldberg, who worked for the city, began to spend evenings sitting outside on the sandstone step in front of our house discussing the problems of the Depression. They blamed the national Republican government and decided to go into politics to find answers. The two friends ran for Democratic committeemen from the 23rd Division of the 30th Ward in South Philadelphia. They won handily and became politically active while still working in their respective jobs.

The pair called their first meeting in my father's big front parlor at 2324 Christian Street. People from the neighborhood came in droves --black, white, immigrants and residents of many years. The meeting was uproarious!

My friend and neighbor, Shangle Goldberg, and I crouched down behind the sofa in our living room watching our fathers and listening to the clash of voices at the meeting. Residents were shouting and demanding answers!

"Why is our food market closing?" "I've lost my job!" people shouted. "How will we pay our bills?" What is this thing called "Relief?" "Who is this guy named Roosevelt?" "Who's in charge of this meeting?"

When order was at last restored, the chairmen recorded concerns, formed committees, and promised grumbling neighbors that the group would meet again at the same location and work to find solutions to the problems!

Shangle and I put our 10-year-old curly brown and black heads together to examine the Street List which had just been distributed. Street Lists contained the names and addresses of local residents who were registered to vote. We decided that we would divide the list, ring doorbells and give out fliers to remind people of the coming meetings, "Help elect Franklin Roosevelt President!"

The residents met vigorously twice a month after that. They demanded that merchants reduce food prices because of the Depression and the loss of jobs. They appealed to the local banks for loans to repay debt. Young people offered to help out, while families looked for work. Drugstore owners were asked to lower prescription prices for pregnant women. People who were seeking part-time jobs placed personal ads in local newspapers.

At one meeting the neighbors planned to raise money for needy families by having a Street Party in the 'back street' behind Christian Street --Montrose Street. They would set up tables and sell hot dogs, cakes, water ice and Kool-Aid. People would play games and buy chances. Shangle and I volunteered to serve food and play records, charging 10 cents a dance!

Every week "Get out the Vote" drives were held in neighborhoods all over the city. People became determined to elect Roosevelt, a Democrat, for President. He promised to help people regardless of color and to increase the number of jobs. Our Division Committee mobilized to get out the vote and we enlisted our friends to put up signs. This would be the first presidential election that we were involved in. We wanted to help!

The year was 1933. The day after the election, the nation waited for the results! The radio blared the news that Franklin Roosevelt had been elected President of the United States of America by a landslide! Our town went crazy; horns honked, whistles blew, people called out of windows: "We won, we won!" Church bells rang! The streets were jammed with people dancing, blowing horns and cheering Roosevelt's name!

Neighbors came running to our house to jump into the car with my family. They hung on the roof and clung to the running boards as we drove off, flying down Broad Street singing with the huge crowd, "Happy Days are Here Again!" At Front Street, we joined the Mummers and the Philadelphia Police Band, marching along the waterfront. Everyone was cheering, singing, clapping and shouting over and over, "Roosevelt for Recovery, Bring Back Prosperity!"

The newly elected Democratic government in Washington awarded my father the position of Director of Fair Employment Practices for the Third District in the state of

Pennsylvania. He held that position while continuing his practice of dentistry. My father spent many happy years establishing programs that provided college scholarships and professional training in the health services for talented African American students in Pennsylvania, paid for by the United States government.

My father also formed an alliance with Sam Evans, who was heavily involved in Philadelphia politics. They had occasion to meet in person with Eleanor Roosevelt to discuss matters of politics and discuss ways in which to move forward as a country during those difficult times.

It was now time for me to go to Junior High School. I had to take a trolley to 46th and Powelton Streets in West Philadelphia to attend Newton Junior High School. The kids at Newton were all races – black, Italian, Irish, Jewish – and I made a lot of friends.

In looking back, the experiences with the diversity in my neighborhood, at school and at camp, shaped the framework of my thinking and that would serve me well throughout my lifetime.

My next step was the Philadelphia High School for Girls, a highly rated, college preparatory school with a superior faculty. The school population was predominately white. I was the only black student in what was referred to as the "Star" section. Our curriculum was challenging – four years of English, Latin, history, mathematics, and a foreign language. The competition was keen. When I finally adjusted to the system of four hours of homework each night, I was off to the races. My classmates and I were bright and eager to learn.

At Girls' High School, a Freshman Prom was announced. My date was our neighbor, Buddy McCoy. I remember wearing a bright pink, ruffled, strapless evening gown and pink slippers! Our transportation was the #7 Public Trolley car, because Buddy's car had begun to "show the street under his feet!" We danced the night away on the Girls' High Roof!

46

That year I was elected Secretary of our class and spent days of "shrewd" negotiation with the other class officers; Olga Michelsavich, Betty Flanagan and Anna Bonneffon! We were all cheerleaders at the exciting gym contest that year. Although we lost, our Bugs Bunny cheers were definitely the most exciting!

Graduation Day came in 1940! My poem, "What is an American?" was chosen, and I proudly read it. Noted author, Pearl S. Buck, was our keynote speaker. I was awarded two four-year scholarships; one was to Sarah Lawrence College and the other to Howard University. I chose Howard because my father had finished Dental School there and my mother had studied to be a teacher there.

The gates of Howard University in our nation's Capital welcomed me like a child coming home. I loved the towering law school, the vine-covered chapel, Truth Hall and the Logan Library! I happily hugged old friends from Camp Atwater and met new friends from across the nation. We all pledged Delta Sigma Theta together, working side by side on service projects and social events. We pledged under our big sister, Patricia Roberts Harris, who was to be the future Housing and Urban Development Secretary under President Jimmy Carter. Secondary English Education and Television Production were my choices for study. I thrilled to the exciting and stimulating college courses taught by great professors like Alain Locke, E. Franklin Frazier, and Sterling Brown.

Among the new friends I met on campus was a handsome dental student from New York and Trinidad, British West Indies, named Norbert Bain, Jr., the son of a Howard Dental School graduate. He was a member of the fraternity Alpha Phi Alpha, pledging under (the future Mayor) David Dinkins of New York. We became close friends and spent many wonderful happy hours on campus with (the future doctors) Les Hayling, Turner Johnson, Fleming H. "Buddy" Norris and (the future Pennsylvania Commonwealth Court Judge) Robert W. "Bobby" Williams, Jr., who was the first

African American to join the Court. We all remained lifelong friends.

Norbert completed four years of Dental School. In 1947, I graduated from Howard with a Bachelor's degree in Education and stayed on to get a Masters in English in 1948.

Norbert proposed and we and moved to Philadelphia to start careers and raise a family. We were married on December 27, 1950. Our wedding reception was at the prestigious Pyramid Club, where Grandfather Grinnage had long been a member. Norbert pursued a lucrative dental practice and was active in family, church, civic and social events.

Our son, Norbert III, was born on December 21, 1953. A year and two months later, his sister, Coralie, was born. The two were inseparable.

Following in his father's footsteps, my husband Norbert pursued a successful dental practice in Center City. In his free time, he read to and doted on his children. He even had several occasions when he treated celebrity patients. On one such occasion, Duke Ellington was referred to him. The Duke was performing in Philadelphia and developed a toothache! Norbert successfully treated him.

I was appointed a teacher of English in the Philadelphia secondary schools. I wrote, directed and hosted television instructional programs: *Books in Action, Story Corner*, and *Three, Four, Open the Door* on WHYY, Philadelphia's public television station and on Channel 3.

Educational TV was just coming of age and we used a variety of instructional materials to help lead into discovery experiences in the classroom. I was the first African American to appear in programs of this nature in the city of Philadelphia. Every spring and summer we worked closely with the Board of Education's curriculum committee to help plan the coming year's course of study in various academic areas.

With *Books in Action*, I was asked to develop a curriculum with the works of black writers. I drafted an outline for a series that would present dramatizations of selected works. (Our relatives, Allan, Phil and Doug Freelon appeared in one memorable episode of Three, Four, Open the Door!) In 1967 I prepared three series of 37 programs each. When it came to vacations, we just didn't get them!

During my career I taught hundreds of students at Fitz-Simons and Barratt Junior High School and went on to become Supervisor of the Board of Education's Radio/Television Division. After two-dozen years of teaching, I was promoted to Curriculum Specialist of the English/ Reading/Language Arts Division, retiring after 33 years with the Philadelphia School District as Assistant Director.

Norbert III and Coralie enjoyed exciting educational opportunities in the Philadelphia School System at preparatory schools like Masterman, Girls' High and Central High School. They became members of Christ Church and St. Michael's with their cousins, Phil, Randi, Greg and Doug Freelon. The Freelons were the first African American family to integrate Christ Church and St. Michael's Episcopal Church in Mt. Airy, and our family became the second. Both families remained there for decades. They also enjoyed many happy years in the Jack and Jill organization with close friends Michelle and Dillon Chew, Sammy Wyche and Kwon Young. Our children also attended Howard University and became teachers in the Philadelphia schools and in other cities.

In 1960, I was a founding member of the Philadelphia chapter of the national organization called the Circle-Lets. The national organization was chartered in 1955 and membership represents a diverse spectrum of African American women sharing the basic tenant of friendship. The motto of the Circle-Lets is "To provide a social outlet and a sisterly relationship among women with similar ideals, interests and goals."

I served as Chapter Secretary for many years and have been a Conclave Committee member and was frequently a member of the club's annual Christmas Party Committee. I also assumed the role of maintaining the official chapter photo albums and recruiting new members. I am also a member of the Philadelphia Chapter of the Links, Inc., two bridge clubs, the Karma Club and the Birthday Club.

Our son met and married Natalie Slaughter in Philadelphia, who continues to work as an Information Technology Specialist at University of Pennsylvania. Norbert and his cousin, Greg Freelon, had a radio program on Temple's radio station called *The Infinite Hourglass*. Before that, the public access television station in Atlanta employed him. He won a local Emmy in Philadelphia for his film project about the men who had graduated from Edison High School having the highest number of lives lost in the Vietnam War out of all of the high schools in the country.

Coralie married Greg Barksdale, a dentist whom she met through friends Bill and Cindy Lightfoot, at Howard University. Greg attended undergraduate and Dental School at Howard University, where Coralie also received her undergraduate and Master's degrees. Greg is a champion golfer and inveterate traveler.

Coralie is a retired reading specialist in the Cheltenham and Philadelphia School Districts who worked with small groups of students to improve reading performance. She conducted staff development and training of teachers, assistants and parent groups. She has given back enormous amounts of time and energy to some very worthy causes while in the workforce and after her retirement.

Upon retirement, Coralie became Vice President of the Board of Directors for the Foundation for the School District of Cheltenham and Vice President of the Board of Directors of Opera North, Inc. In addition, she is a member of the Helen O. Dickens Women's Auxiliary at Abington/Jefferson Hospital for which she co-chaired a fundraiser. She is also a past Vice President of the Cheltenham African American Alliance and a former member of the Philadelphia Chapter of the Links, Inc. Her fundraiser for the Links group called "A

Progressive Evening" at the Woodmere Art Museum and Springside School won a regional Links award.

An active member of the Philadelphia Chapter of the Circle-Lets, Coralie has served as the President, Vice President and Secretary of that group. She was also elected National Recording Secretary. Willadine, Coralie and Greg enjoy attending National Conclaves in July where we reconnect with our Circle-Lets friends Cindy Lightfoot, Enid Johnson, Crystal Brown, Lisa Cooper-Hudgins, Betty Dixon, Shawne Thorne and our cousin Betty Bain Pearsall.

Norbert Sr. enjoyed playing a role in the lives of his grandchildren until he passed in 1999 at the age of 73.

Coralie's son, Greg, is a Temple Fox School of Business graduate who is employed by the Defense Logistics Agency. He received his Master's degree in the Science of Business Administration from Central Michigan University. Rachel, our son's daughter, attended Howard University and Temple University.

In 2015 I moved to the historic Stapeley Mansion in Germantown known as Wesley Enhanced Living at Stapeley, where I made new friends. Our family now attends Bethlehem Baptist Church in Spring House, Pennsylvania.

The solid gold necklace purchased by my Grandmother Adele Jones when she was a teacher in Savannah, has been worn by my mother, Mildred, by me, and my daughter, Coralie – who have all served as teachers. Wearing the necklace reminds us of our family's history of serving more than 100 years in the field of education.

Howard University played a major role in shaping us to serve others and our community over these many years.
This is a salute to all of our delightful and accomplished family members – past and present. May our history bring hope and inspiration to our readers!

~Willadine Bain

Pictured: Phil Freelon and Willadine Bain